COOKIE DOUGH FUN

Flip through the pages of this delightful cookbook and see all the wonderful ways to use cookie dough. Set aside some time, perhaps the next rainy day to do projects with your family. Use the suggestions and photos as a starting point and let your imagination go wild! Feel free to change the colors or shapes to suit your family or party.

General Guidelines

- Measure all the ingredients and assemble them in the order called for in the recipe.

- All cookie dough should be well chilled before using. Unless the recipe states otherwise, work with the recommended portion of dough called for and refrigerate the remaining dough until needed.

- Follow recipe directions and baking times. Check for doneness using the test given in the recipe.

- Most refrigerated cookie dough expands considerably when baked. Always leave two inches between cookies when placing them on cookie sheets.

Supplies:

Some of the recipes in *Cookie Dough Fun* call for special equipment or nonfood items; these are always listed in the recipe under the heading "Supplies." Most of the supplies listed are available in stores carrying cake decorating equipment and in supermarkets.

Kitchen Equipment:

Equipment not listed under "Supplies" are things that are normally found in a well-equipped kitchen including: mixing bowls, cookie and baking sheets, rolling pins, small, medium and large saucepans, aluminum foil, waxed paper and cookie cutters.

Additional equipment you may need that is listed under "Supplies" includes: pastry brush, lollipop sticks, cardboard and pastry bags and decorating tips.

Special Techniques

Making Patterns:

When a pattern is to be used only once, as for the Gingerbread Log Cabin, make the pattern out of waxed paper. Using the diagram(s) and photo as guides, draw the pattern pieces on waxed paper. Cut the pieces out and place them on the cookie. Cut around the pattern pieces with a sharp knife. Remove the pattern pieces and discard. Continue as directed in the recipe.

For patterns that are used more than once, make the pattern more durable by using clean lightweight cardboard or poster board. Using the diagram(s) and photo as guides, draw the pattern pieces on the cardboard. Cut the pieces out and lightly spray one side with nonstick cooking spray. Place the pattern pieces, sprayed side down, on the rolled-out dough and cut around them with a sharp knife. Reuse the pattern pieces to make as many cutouts as needed.

Tinting Coconut:

Dilute a few drops of food color with ½ teaspoon water in a large plastic food storage bag. Add 1 to 1⅓ cups flaked coconut. Close the bag and shake well until the coconut is evenly coated. If a deeper color is desired, add more diluted food color and shake again.

Melting Chocolate:

When melting chocolate be sure the utensils are completely dry. Any drop of moisture makes the chocolate become stiff and grainy. If this does happen, add ½ teaspoon shortening (not butter) for each ounce of chocolate and stir until smooth. Chocolate scorches easily, and once scorched cannot be used. Use one of the following three methods for successful melting.

Double Boiler: Place the chocolate in the top of a double boiler or in a heatproof bowl over hot, not boiling water. Stir until smooth. (Make sure the water remains just below a simmer and is one inch below the top pan.) Be careful that no steam or water gets into the chocolate.

Direct Heat: Place the chocolate in a heavy saucepan and melt over very low heat, stirring constantly. Remove the chocolate from the heat as soon as it is melted. Be sure to watch the chocolate carefully since it is easily scorched with this method.

Microwave Oven: Place a 1-ounce square of chocolate or 1 cup of chocolate chips in a small microwavable bowl. Microwave on HIGH 1 to 2 minutes or until the chocolate is almost melted, stirring well after every minute. Add 10 seconds for each additional ounce of chocolate. Be sure to stir the microwaved chocolate well because it retains its original shape even when melted.

"Everything but the Kitchen Sink" Bar Cookies

What you need:

1 package
(18 ounces)
refrigerated
chocolate chip
cookie dough
1 jar (7 ounces)
marshmallow
creme
½ cup creamy peanut
butter
1½ cups toasted corn
cereal
½ cup miniature
candy-coated
chocolate pieces

1 Preheat oven to 350°F.
Grease 13×9-inch baking
pan. Remove dough from
wrapper according to
package directions.

2 Press dough into
prepared baking pan.
Bake 13 minutes.

3 Remove baking pan from
oven. Drop teaspoonfuls
of marshmallow creme and
peanut butter over hot cookie
base.

4 Bake 1 minute. Carefully
spread marshmallow
creme and peanut butter over
cookie base.

5 Sprinkle cereal and
chocolate pieces over
melted marshmallow and
peanut butter mixture.

6 Bake 7 minutes. Cool
completely on wire rack.
Cut into 2-inch bars.
Makes 3 dozen bar cookies

**"Everything but the Kitchen
Sink" Bar Cookies**

Sandwich Cookies

What you need:

1 package (20 ounces) refrigerated cookie dough, any flavor
All-purpose flour (optional)

FILLINGS

Any combination of colored frostings, peanut butter or assorted ice creams

DECORATIONS

Colored sprinkles, chocolate-covered raisins, miniature candy-coated chocolate pieces and other assorted small candies

1 Preheat oven to 350°F. Grease cookie sheets.

2 Remove dough from wrapper according to package directions.

3 Cut dough into 4 equal sections. Reserve 1 section; refrigerate remaining 3 sections.

4 Roll reserved dough to ¼-inch thickness. Sprinkle with flour to minimize sticking, if necessary.

5 Cut out cookies using 1 (¾-inch) round cookie cutter. Transfer cookies to prepared cookie sheets, placing about 2 inches apart. Repeat steps with remaining dough.

6 Bake 8 to 11 minutes or until edges are lightly browned. Remove to wire racks cool completely.

7 To make sandwich, spread about 1 tablespoon desire filling to within ¼-inch of the underside of 1 cookie. Top with second cookie, pressing gently.

8 Roll side of sandwich in desired decorations. Repeat with remaining cookies. *Makes about 20 to 24 sandwic cookie*

Be creative—make sandwich cookies using 2 or more flavors c refrigerated cookie dough. Mix and match to see how many flavc combinations you can come up with.

Chocolate Malted Cookies

What you need:

½ **cup butter or**
    margarine, softened
½ **cup shortening**
1¾ **cups powdered sugar,**
    divided
1 **teaspoon vanilla**
2 **cups all-purpose flour**
1 **cup malted milk**
    powder, divided
¼ **cup unsweetened**
    cocoa powder

1 Beat butter, shortening, ¾ cup powdered sugar and vanilla in large bowl at high speed of electric mixer.

2 Add flour, ½ cup malted milk powder and cocoa; beat at low speed until well blended. Refrigerate several hours or overnight.

3 Preheat oven to 350°F. Shape slightly mounded teaspoonfuls of dough into balls.

4 Place dough balls about 2 inches apart on ungreased cookie sheets.

5 Bake 14 to 16 minutes or until lightly browned.

6 Meanwhile, combine remaining 1 cup powdered sugar and ½ cup malted milk powder in medium bowl.

7 Remove cookies to wire racks; cool 5 minutes. Roll cookies in powdered sugar mixture.

Makes about 4 dozen cookie

Substitute 6 ounces melted semisweet chocolate for the 1 cu powdered sugar and ½ cup malted milk powder used to roll the cookies. Instead, dip cookies in melted chocolate and let dry o wire racks until coating is set.

Peanuts

What you need:

½ cup butter or
    margarine, softened
¼ cup shortening
¼ cup creamy peanut
    butter
1 cup powdered sugar,
    sifted
1 egg yolk
1 teaspoon vanilla
1¾ cups all-purpose flour
1 cup finely ground
    honey-roasted
    peanuts, divided
    Peanut Buttery
    Frosting (recipe
    follows)

1 Grease cookie sheets.

2 Beat butter, shortening and peanut butter in large bowl at medium speed of electric mixer. Gradually add powdered sugar, beating until smooth. Add egg yolk and vanilla; beat well. Add flour; mix well. Stir in ⅓ cup ground peanuts. Cover dough; refrigerate 1 hour.

3 Prepare Peanut Buttery Frosting. Preheat oven to 350°F. Shape dough into 1-inch balls. Place 2 balls, side by side and slightly touching, on prepared cookie sheet. Gently flatten balls with fingertips and form into "peanut" shape. Repeat steps with remaining dough.

4 Bake 16 to 18 minutes or until edges are lightly browned. Cool on cookie sheet 5 minutes. Remove cookies to wire racks; cool completely.

5 Place remaining ⅔ cup ground peanuts in shallow dish. Spread about 2 teaspoons Peanut Buttery Frosting evenly over top of each cookie. Coat with ground peanuts.
Makes about 2 dozen cookies

Peanut Buttery Frosting

½ cup butter or margarine,
    softened
½ cup creamy peanut
    butter
2 cups powdered sugar,
    sifted
½ teaspoon vanilla
3 to 6 tablespoons milk

1 Beat butter and peanut butter in medium bowl at medium speed of electric mixer until smooth. Gradually add powdered sugar and vanilla until blended but crumbly.

2 Add milk, 1 tablespoon at a time, until smooth. Refrigerate until ready to use.
Makes 1⅓ cups frosting

Butter Pretzel Cookies

1 recipe Butter Cookie Dough (page 92)

TOPPINGS
   White, rainbow or colored rock or coarse sugar

1 Prepare Butter Cookie Dough. Cover; refrigerate about 4 hours or until firm.

2 Preheat oven to 350°F. Grease cookie sheets.

3 Divide dough into 4 equal sections. Reserve 1 section; refrigerate remaining 3 sections. Divide reserved dough into 4 equal pieces. Roll each dough piece on lightly floured surface to 12-inch rope; sprinkle with rock or coarse sugar.

4 Transfer 1 rope at a time to prepared cookie sheets. Form each rope into pretzel shape. Repeat steps with remaining dough pieces.

5 Bake 14 to 18 minutes or until edges begin to brown. Cool cookies on cookie sheets 1 minute. Remove to wire racks; cool completely.

Makes 16 cookies

Chocolate Pretzel Cookies

1 recipe Chocolate Cookie Dough (page 92)

TOPPINGS
   White and colored rock or coarse sugar

1 Prepare Chocolate Cookie Dough. Cover; refrigerate about 2 hours or until firm.

2 Preheat oven to 325°F. Grease cookie sheets.

3 Divide dough into 4 equal sections. Reserve 1 section; refrigerate remaining 3 sections. Divide reserved dough into 5 equal pieces. Roll each dough piece on lightly floured surface to 12-inch rope; sprinkle with rock or coarse sugar.

4 Transfer 1 rope at a time to prepared cookie sheets. Form each rope into pretzel shape. Repeat steps with remaining dough pieces.

5 Bake 12 to 14 minutes or until edges begin to brown. Cool cookies on cookie sheets 1 minute. Remove to wire racks; cool completely.

Makes 20 cookies

Surprise Cookies

What you need:

**1 package (20 ounces)
refrigerated sugar
cookie dough
All-purpose flour
(optional)**

FILLINGS

**Any combination of
walnut halves, whole
almonds, chocolate-
covered raisins or
caramel candy
squares**

1 Grease cookie sheets.
Remove dough from
wrapper according to package
directions.

2 Cut dough into 4 equal
sections. Reserve
1 section; refrigerate remaining
3 sections.

3 Roll reserved dough to
¼-inch thickness. Sprinkle
with flour to minimize sticking, if
necessary.

4 Cut out 3-inch square
cookie with sharp knife.
Transfer cookie to prepared
cookie sheet.

5 Place desired "surprise"
filling in center of cookie. (If
using caramel candy square,
place so that caramel forms
diamond shape within square).

6 Bring up 4 corners of
dough towards center;
pinch gently to seal. Repeat
steps with remaining dough and
fillings, placing cookies about
2 inches apart.

7 Freeze cookies 20 minutes.
Preheat oven to 350°F.

8 Bake 9 to 11 minutes or
until edges are lightly
browned. Remove to wire racks;
cool completely.

Makes about 14 cookies

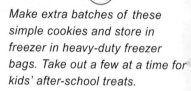

Tip

*Make extra batches of these
simple cookies and store in
freezer in heavy-duty freezer
bags. Take out a few at a time for
kids' after-school treats.*

Fruity Cookie Rings and Twists

What you need:

1 package (20 ounces) refrigerated sugar cookie dough
3 cups fruit-flavored cereal, crushed, divided

1 Remove dough from wrapper according to package directions.

2 Combine dough and ½ cup cereal in large bowl. Divide dough into 32 balls. Refrigerate 1 hour.

3 Preheat oven to 375°F. Roll dough balls into 6- to 8-inch-long ropes. Roll ropes in remaining cereal to coat; shape into rings or fold in half and twist.

4 Place cookies 2 inches apart on ungreased cookie sheets.

5 Bake 10 to 11 minutes or until lightly browned. Remove to wire racks; cool completely.

Makes 32 cookie

Tip

These cookie rings can be transformed into Christmas tree ornaments by poking a hole in the unbaked ring using a drinking straw. Bake cookies and decorate with colored gels and small candies to resemble wreaths. Loop thin ribbon through holes and tie together.

Pecan Toffee Filled Ravioli Cookies

What you need:

1 cup packed brown
    sugar
¼ cup butter, melted
½ cup chopped pecans
2 tablespoons all-
    purpose flour
2 recipes Butter Cookie
    Dough (page 92)

1 Stir brown sugar into melted butter in large bowl until well blended. Add pecans and flour; mix well.

2 Transfer filling to waxed paper; shape into 7-inch square.

3 Cut into 36 (1¼-inch) pieces. Refrigerate 1 hour or overnight.

4 Prepare Butter Cookie Dough. Cover; refrigerate about 4 hours or until firm. Roll half of dough on well-floured sheet of waxed paper to 12-inch square.

5 Repeat with second half of dough. If dough becomes soft, refrigerate 1 hour.

6 Preheat oven to 350°F. Lightly score 1 layer of dough at 2 inch intervals to form 36 squares.

7 Place 1 square of brown sugar filling in center of each square.

8 Carefully place second layer of dough over brown sugar mixture. Press gently between rows. Cut with knife, ravioli wheel or pastry cutter.

9 Transfer filled ravioli to ungreased cookie sheets.

10 Bake 14 to 16 minutes or until lightly browned. Cool on cookie sheets 5 minutes. Remove to wire racks; cool completely.
        Makes 3 dozen cookie

(Tip)

For a fun flavor adventure, fill ravioli cookies with 1-inch squares of semisweet or milk chocolate instead of brown sugar pecan mixture. Omit steps 1 through 3.

**Pecan Toffee Filled Ravioli
Cookies**

Peanut Butter and Chocolate Spirals

What you need:

1 package (20 ounces)
   refrigerated sugar
   cookie dough
1 package (20 ounces)
   refrigerated peanut
   butter cookie dough
¼ cup unsweetened
   cocoa powder
⅓ cup peanut butter-
   flavored chips,
   chopped
¼ cup all-purpose flour
⅓ cup miniature
   chocolate chips

1 Remove each dough from wrapper according to package directions.

2 Place sugar cookie dough and cocoa in large bowl; mix with fork to blend. Stir in peanut butter chips.

3 Place peanut butter cookie dough and flour in another large bowl; mix with fork to blend. Stir in chocolate chips. Divide each dough in half; refrigerate 1 hour.

4 Roll each dough on floured surface to 6×12-inch rectangle. Layer each half of peanut butter dough onto each half of chocolate dough. Roll up dough, starting at long end to form 2 (12-inch) rolls. Refrigerate 1 hour.

5 Preheat oven to 375°F. Cut dough into ½-inch-thick slices. Place cookies 2 inches apart on ungreased cookie sheets.

6 Bake 10 to 12 minutes or until lightly browned. Remove to wire racks; cool completely.

Makes 4 dozen cookies

Apple Pie Wedges

What you need:

1 cup butter, softened
²⁄₃ cup sugar
1 egg yolk
¹⁄₃ cup apple butter
2¹⁄₃ cups all-purpose flour
1 teaspoon ground
cinnamon
½ teaspoon apple pie
spice
½ teaspoon vanilla

1 Beat butter and sugar in medium bowl at medium speed of electric mixer until fluffy.

2 Add egg yolk and apple butter; mix well. Add flour, cinnamon, apple pie spice and vanilla; beat at low speed until well blended.

3 Divide dough in half. Shape each half into a 6-inch disc on waxed paper. Refrigerate 30 minutes.

4 Preheat oven to 325°F. Invert 1 disc of dough into ungreased 9-inch round pie plate.

5 Press dough into plate with lightly floured hand covering plate completely.

6 Flute edges using handle of wooden spoon. Deeply score into 8 wedges.

7 Prick surface using tines of fork. Repeat steps with remaining disc of dough and another pie plate.

8 Bake 35 minutes or until golden brown. Remove to wire rack; cool completely. Cut into wedges.

Makes 16 wedges

Serve these tasty cookies warm with a big scoop of vanilla or cinnamon-flavored ice cream.

Kids' Cookie Dough

What you need:

1 cup butter, softened
2 teaspoons vanilla
½ cup powdered sugar
2¼ cups all-purpose flour
¼ teaspoon salt

DECORATIONS
Assorted colored glazes, frostings, sugars and small candies

1 Preheat oven to 350°F. Grease cookie sheets.

2 Beat butter and vanilla in large bowl at high speed of electric mixer until fluffy. Add sugar and beat at medium speed until blended.

3 Combine flour and salt in small bowl. Gradually add to butter mixture.

4 Divide dough into 10 equal sections. Form shapes directly on prepared cookie sheets according to photo, or as desired, for each section.

5 Bake 15 to 18 minutes or until edges are lightly browned. Cool completely on cookie sheets.

6 Decorate with glazes, frostings, sugars and small candies as desired.
Makes 10 (4-inch) cookies

Kids' Cookie Dough

Diamond Backs

**1 recipe Gingerbread
Cookie Dough
(page 91)**

DECORATIONS
2 egg yolks
½ teaspoon water
**Assorted paste food
colors**

SUPPLIES
**Small craft paint
brushes**

1 Prepare Gingerbread
Cookie Dough. Cover;
refrigerate about 8 hours or until
firm.

2 Combine egg yolks and
water in small bowl. Divide
egg mixture evenly among small
custard cups. Add different food
colors to each cup; blend well.
Set aside.

3 Preheat oven to 350°F.
Grease cookie sheets.

4 Divide dough in half.
Reserve 1 half; refrigerate
remaining dough. Roll reserved
dough into rectangle on floured
surface to ¼-inch thickness.

5 Cut dough into squiggly
8×1-inch strips for bodies,
leaving one end pointed.
Carefully transfer to prepared
cookie sheets.

6 Reroll scraps to ¼-inch
thickness; cut into 1½-inch
teardrop shapes for heads.

7 Paint bodies of diamond
backs as desired using
small craft paint brushes and
egg yolk paint.

8 Place teardrop heads on
bodies; press gently.
Decorate according to photo or
as desired. Repeat with
remaining dough.

9 Bake 12 to 13 minutes or
until set. Cool on cookie
sheets 5 minutes. Remove to
wire racks; cool completely.
Makes about 14 cookie

Tip

*Using paste food color for
diamond backs is not absolutely
necessary, but it can give better
results by producing bright vibran
hues. Also, it will not thin the egg
yolk mixture like liquid food color.*

Cookie Canvases

What you need:

1 package (20 ounces) refrigerated cookie dough, any flavor
All-purpose flour (optional)
1 recipe Cookie Glaze (page 94)

SUPPLIES
1 (3½-inch) square cardboard template
1 (2½×4½-inch) rectangular cardboard template
Assorted liquid food colors
Small craft paint brushes

1 Preheat oven to 350°F. Grease cookie sheets.

2 Remove dough from wrapper according to package directions. Cut dough in half. Wrap half of dough in plastic wrap and refrigerate.

3 Roll remaining dough on floured surface to ¼-inch thickness. Sprinkle with flour to minimize sticking, if necessary. Cut out cookie shapes using cardboard templates as guides. Place cookies 2 inches apart on prepared cookie sheets. Repeat steps with remaining dough.

4 Bake 8 to 10 minutes or until edges are lightly browned. Remove from oven and straighten cookie edges with spatula. Cool cookies completely on cookie sheets. Prepare Cookie Glaze.

5 Place cookies on wire racks set over waxed paper. Drizzle Cookie Glaze over cookies. Let stand at room temperature 40 minutes or until glaze is set. Place food colors in small bowls. Using small craft paint brushes, decorate cookies with food colors by "painting" designs such as rainbows, flowers and animals.

Makes 8 to 10 cookie canvases

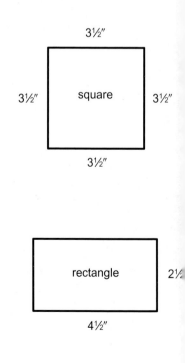

Thumbprints

What you need:

**1 package (20 ounces)
refrigerated sugar or
chocolate cookie
dough
All-purpose flour
(optional)
¾ cup plus 1 tablespoon
fruit preserves, any
flavor**

1 Grease cookie sheets.

2 Remove dough from wrapper according to package directions. Sprinkle with flour to minimize sticking, if necessary.

3 Cut dough into 26 (1-inch) slices. Roll slices into balls, sprinkling with additional flour, if necessary.

4 Place balls 2 inches apart on prepared cookie sheets.

5 Press deep indention in center of each ball with thumb.

6 Freeze dough 20 minutes. Preheat oven to 350°F.

7 Bake cookies 12 to 13 minutes or until edges are light golden brown (cookies wi' have started to puff up and loose their shape). Quickly press down indentation using of teaspoon.

8 Return to oven 2 to 3 minutes or until cookies a golden brown and set.

9 Cool cookies completely cookie sheets.

10 Fill each indentation with about 1½ teaspoons preserves.

Makes 26 cookie

Tip

These cookies are filled with frui preserves, but they would be jus as delicious filled with peanut butter or melted semisweet chocolate chips.

Cookie Clocks

What you need:

1 package (20 ounces) refrigerated cookie dough, any flavor
All-purpose flour (optional)

DECORATIONS
Colored and white frostings and assorted candies

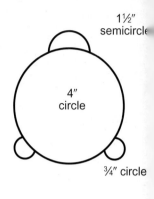

1½" semicircle

4" circle

¾" circle

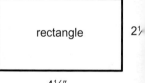

rectangle

2½

4½"

1 Preheat oven to 350°F. Grease cookie sheets.

2 Remove dough from wrapper according to package directions. Cut dough into 4 equal sections. Reserve 1 section; refrigerate remaining 3 sections. Sprinkle reserved dough with flour to minimize sticking, if necessary. Roll dough to ¼-inch thickness.

3 Cut out various shapes of clocks and watches using diagrams as guides. Carefully place cookies 2 inches apart on prepared cookie sheets. Repeat steps with remaining dough.

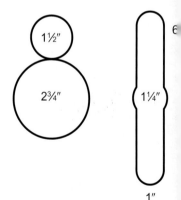

1½"

2¾"

6

1¼"

1"

4 Bake 8 to 10 minutes or until edges are lightly browned. Cool cookies on cookie sheets 5 minutes. Remove to wire racks; cool completely. Decorate as desired.

Makes about 8 to 10 cookies

Handprints

What you need:

**1 package (20 ounces)
refrigerated cookie
dough, any flavor
All-purpose flour
(optional)**

**DECORATIONS
Cookie glazes,
frostings, nondairy
whipped topping,
peanut butter and
assorted candies**

1 Grease cookie sheets.

2 Remove dough from wrapper according to package directions.

3 Cut dough into 4 equal sections. Reserve 1 section; refrigerate remaining 3 sections. Sprinkle reserved dough with flour to minimize sticking, if necessary.

4 Roll dough on prepared cookie sheet to 5×7-inch rectangle.

5 Place hand, palm-side down, on dough. Carefully, cut around outline of hand with knife. Remove scraps. Separate fingers as much as possible using small spatula. Pat fingers outward to lengthen slightly. Repeat steps with remaining dough.

6 Freeze dough 15 minutes. Preheat oven to 350°F.

7 Bake 7 to 13 minutes or until cookies are set and edges are golden brown. Cool completely on cookie sheets.

8 Decorate as desired.
Makes 5 adult handprint cooki

Tip

*To get the kids involved, let then
use their hands to make the
handprints. Be sure that an adul
is available to cut around the
outline with a knife. The kids will
enjoy seeing how their handprint
bake into big cookies.*

Chocolate Teddy Bears

What you need:

1 recipe Chocolate Cookie Dough (page 92)

DECORATIONS
White and colored frostings, decorator gels, coarse sugars and assorted small candies

1 Prepare Chocolate Cookie Dough. Cover; refrigerate about 2 hours or until firm.

2 Preheat oven to 325°F. Grease cookie sheets.

3 Divide dough in half. Reserve 1 half; refrigerate remaining dough.

4 Divide reserved dough into 8 equal balls. Cut 1 ball in half; roll 1 half into ball for body.

5 Cut other half into 2 equal pieces; roll 1 piece into 4 small balls for paws.

6 Divide second piece into thirds. Roll two-thirds of dough into ball for head.

7 Divide remaining one-third of dough in half; roll into 2 small balls for ears.

8 Place balls together to form bear according to diagram directly on prepared cookie sheet. Repeat steps with remaining dough.

9 Bake 13 to 15 minutes or until set. Cool completely on cookie sheets. Decorate with frostings, gels, sugars and assorted candies as desired.
Makes 16 (4-inch) teddy bears

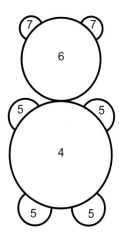

Numbers in diagram refer to steps recipe.

Puzzle Cookie

What you need:

¾ cup shortening
½ cup packed light
  brown sugar
6 tablespoons dark
  molasses
2 egg whites
¾ teaspoon vanilla
2¼ cups all-purpose flour
¾ teaspoon baking soda
¼ teaspoon plus
  ⅛ teaspoon baking
  powder
¾ teaspoon salt
2 teaspoons ground
  cinnamon
¾ teaspoon ground
  ginger

DECORATIONS
  Assorted colored
  frostings, colored
  sugars, colored
  decorator gels and
  assorted small
  candies

1 Beat shortening, brown sugar, molasses, egg whites and vanilla in large bowl at high speed of electric mixer until smooth.

2 Combine flour, baking soda, baking powder, salt, cinnamon and ginger in medium bowl. Add to shortening mixture; mix well. Shape dough into flat rectangle. Wrap in plastic wrap and refrigerate about 8 hours or until firm.

3 Preheat oven to 350°F. Grease jelly-roll pan.

4 Sprinkle dough with additional flour. Place dough in center of prepared p and roll evenly to within ½ inch of edge of pan. Cut shapes in dough according to photo, usir cookie cutters or free-hand, allowing at least 1 inch betwee each shape. Cut through doug using sharp knife, but do not remove cookie shapes.

5 Bake 12 minutes or until edges begin to brown lightly. Remove from oven and retrace shapes with knife. Return to oven 5 to 6 minutes. Cool in pan 5 minutes. Careful remove shapes to wire racks; cool completely.

6 Decorate shapes with frostings, sugars, decorato gels and small candies as shown in photo. Leave puzzle frame in pan. Decorate with frostings, colored sugars and gels to represent sky, clouds, grass and water, if desired. Return shapes to their respective openings to complet puzzle.

*Makes 1 (15×10-inch) puzz.
cook.*

Critters-in-Holes

What you need:

48 chewy caramel candies coated in milk chocolate
48 pieces candy corn
Miniature candy-coated chocolate pieces
1 container frosting, any flavor
1 package (20 ounces) refrigerated peanut butter cookie dough

1 Cut slit into side of 1 caramel candy using sharp knife.

2 Carefully insert 1 piece candy corn into slit. Repeat with remaining caramel candies and candy corn.

3 Attach miniature chocolate pieces to caramel candies to resemble "eyes" using frosting as glue. Decorate as desired.

4 Preheat oven to 350°F. Grease 12 (1¾-inch) muffin cups.

5 Remove dough from wrapper according to package directions. Cut dough into 12 (1-inch) slices. Cut each slice into 4 equal sections. Place 1 section of dough into each muffin cup.

6 Bake 9 minutes. Remove from oven and immediately press 1 decorated caramel candy into center of each cookie. Repeat with remaining ingredients.

7 Remove to wire racks; cool completely.
Makes 4 dozen cookies

Critters-in-Holes

Rainbows

What you need:

1 recipe Christmas Ornament Cookie Dough (page 93)
Red, green, yellow and blue paste food colors

DECORATIONS
White frosting and gold glitter dust

1 Prepare Christmas Ornament Cookie Dough. Divide dough into 10 equal sections. Combine 4 sections dough and red food coloring in large bowl; blend until smooth.

2 Combine 3 sections dough and green food coloring in medium bowl; blend until smooth.

3 Combine 2 sections dough and yellow food coloring in another medium bowl; blend until smooth.

4 Combine remaining dough and blue food coloring in small bowl; blend until smooth. Wrap each section of dough in plastic wrap. Refrigerate 30 minutes.

5 Shape blue dough into 8-inch log. Shape yellow dough into 8×3-inch rectangle; place on waxed paper. Place blue log in center of yellow rectangle. Fold yellow edges up and around blue log, pinching to seal. Roll to form smooth log.

6 Roll green dough into 8×5 inch rectangle on waxed paper. Place yellow log in center of green rectangle. Fold green edges up and around yellow log. Pinch to seal. Roll gently to form smooth log.

7 Roll red dough into 8×7-inch rectangle. Place green log in center of red rectangle. Fold red edges up and around green log. Pinch to seal. Roll gently to form smooth log. Wrap in plastic wrap. Refrigerate 1 hour.

8 Preheat oven to 350°F. Grease cookie sheets. Cut log in half lengthwise. Cut each half into ¼-inch-thick slices. Place slices 1 inch apart on prepared cookie sheets. Bake 8 to 12 minutes. (Do not brown.) Cool on cookie sheets 1 minute. Remove to wire racks; cool completely.

9 Pipe small amount of frosting on bottom corner of 1 side of each cookie and sprinkle with glitter dust. Let stand 1 hour or until frosting sets.

Makes about 5 dozen cookies

Domino Cookies

What you need:

**1 package (20 ounces)
refrigerated sugar
cookie dough
All-purpose flour
(optional)
½ cup semisweet
chocolate chips**

1 Preheat oven to 350°F.
Grease cookie sheets.

2 Remove dough from
wrapper according to
package directions. Cut dough
into 4 equal sections. Reserve
1 section; refrigerate remaining
3 sections.

3 Roll reserved dough to
⅛-inch thickness. Sprinkle
with flour to minimize sticking, if
necessary.

4 Cut out 9 (1¾×2½-inch)
rectangles according to
diagram using sharp knife.
Place 2 inches apart on
prepared cookies sheets.

5 Score each cookie across
middle with sharp knife.

6 Gently press chocolate
chips, point side down, into
dough to resemble various
dominos. Repeat with remaining
dough and scraps.

 Bake 8 to 10 minutes or
until edges are light golden
brown. Remove to wire racks;
cool completely.

Makes 36 cookies

Tip

*Use these adorable cookies as a
learning tool for kids. They can
count the number of chocolate
chips in each cookie and arrange
them in lots of ways: highest to
lowest, numerically or even solve
simple math problems. As a treat
they can eat the cookies
afterwards.*

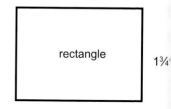

rectangle

1¾"

2½"

Honey Bees

What you need:

¾ cup shortening
½ cup sugar
¼ cup honey
1 egg
½ teaspoon vanilla
2 cups all-purpose flour
⅓ cup cornmeal
1 teaspoon baking
    powder
½ teaspoon salt

DECORATIONS
Yellow and black
    icings or gels and
    gummy fruit

1 Beat shortening, sugar and honey in large bowl at medium speed of electric mixer until fluffy. Add egg and vanilla; mix until well blended.

2 Combine flour, cornmeal, baking powder and salt in medium bowl. Add to shortening mixture; mix at low speed until well blended.

3 Cover; refrigerate several hours or overnight, if desired.

4 Preheat oven to 375°F. Divide dough into 24 equal sections.

5 Shape each section into oval-shaped ball. Place 2 inches apart on ungreased cookie sheets.

6 Bake 10 to 12 minutes or until lightly browned. Cool 2 minutes on cookie sheets. Remove to wire racks; cool completely.

7 Decorate with icings, gels and gummy fruit to create honey bees.

Makes 2 dozen cookie

Tip

To create a summer flower cookie garden, pair these light sweet Honey Bees with a batch of Nutty Sunflower Cookies (page 50) and Rainbows (page 42).

Hot Dog Cookies

What you need:

**1 recipe Butter Cookie
   Dough (page 92)
Liquid food colors
Sesame seeds**

TOPPINGS
   **Shredded coconut, red
   and green decorator
   gels, frosting and
   gummy candies**

1 Prepare Butter Cookie
Dough. Cover; refrigerate
4 hours or until firm. Grease
cookie sheets.

2 Use ⅓ of dough to make
"hot dogs." Refrigerate
remaining dough. Mix food
colors in small bowl to get
reddish-brown color following
chart on back of food color box.
Add reserved ⅓ of dough. Mix
color throughout dough using
wooden spoon.

3 Divide colored dough into
6 equal sections. Roll each
section into thin log shape.
Round edges. Set aside.

4 To make "buns," divide
remaining dough into
6 equal sections.

5 Roll sections into thick logs.
Make very deep indentation
the length of log in centers;
smooth edges to create buns.

6 Lift buns with small spatula
and dip sides in sesame
seeds. Place 3 inches apart on
prepared cookie sheets.

7 Place hot dogs inside buns.

8 Freeze 20 minutes. Preheat
oven to 350°F. Bake 17 to
20 minutes or until bun edges
are light golden brown. Cool
completely on cookie sheets.

9 Top hot dogs with green-
tinted shredded coconut for
"relish," white coconut for
"onions," red decorator gel for
"ketchup" and yellow-tinted
frosting or whipped topping for
"mustard."

Makes 6 hot dog cookies.

Tip

*To pipe gels and frosting onto Hot
Dog Cookies, you can use a
resealable plastic sandwich bag
as a substitute for a pastry bag.
Fold the top of the bag down to
form a cuff and use a spatula to
fill bag half full with gel or
frosting. Unfold top of bag and
twist down against filling. Snip tiny
tip off one corner of bag. Hold
top of bag tightly and squeeze
filling through opening.*

Nutty Sunflower Cookies

What you need:

**1 package (20 ounces)
    refrigerated peanut
    butter cookie dough
⅓ cup all-purpose flour
½ cup semisweet
    chocolate chips
½ cup unsalted
    sunflower seeds**

**DECORATIONS
    Yellow and green icing**

1 Remove dough from wrapper according to package directions. Combine dough and flour in large bowl; mix well with wooden spoon.

2 Divide dough into 8 equal sections. Preheat oven to 375°F.

3 For each sunflower, divide 1 dough section in half. Roll one half into ball; flatten on ungreased cookie sheet to 2½-inch thickness.

4 Roll other half into 5-inch long rope. Cut 2 inches from rope for stem.

5 Cut remaining 3 inches into 10 equal sections; roll into small balls.

6 Arrange stem and small balls around large ball according to photo on cookie sheet. Repeat with remaining dough.

7 Bake 10 to 11 minutes or until lightly browned. Cool 4 minutes on cookie sheets. Remove to wire racks; cool completely.

8 Melt chocolate chips in microwavable bowl at HIGH (100%) 1½ minutes or until smooth, stirring after 1 minute.

9 Spread melted chocolate in center of each cookie; sprinkle with sunflower seeds.

10 Decorate petals with yellow icing according to photo. Decorate stem with green icing or additional melted chocolate, if desired.

Makes 8 cookies

Gingerbread Farm Animals in Corral

What you need:

1 recipe Gingerbread House Dough (page 93)
2 recipes Royal Icing (page 94)

DECORATIONS
Assorted food colors
Shredded coconut
Assorted small hard candies

SUPPLIES
Cardboard
Decorative paper

1 Preheat oven to 375°F. Prepare Gingerbread House Dough. Divide dough into 4 equal sections. To make fence, roll 1 section of dough directly onto large cookie sheet to ¼-inch thickness. Cut into 6 (2¾×6-inch) sections, leaving ½-inch space between sections. Bake 10 to 12 minutes or until edges are browned. Cool completely on wire racks.

2 Roll second section of dough directly onto cookie sheet to ¼-inch thickness. Cut into 4 (2¾×6-inch) sections and 2 (3-inch) sections. Bake 10 to 12 minutes or until edges are browned. Cool completely on wire racks.

3 To make animals, roll remaining 2 sections of dough directly on cookie sheets to ⅛-inch thickness. Cut out animal shapes using animal-shaped cookie cutters. Bake 8 to 12 minutes or until edges are browned. Cool completely on wire racks.

4 Prepare Royal Icing. Tint small amounts of icing with food colors to decorate animals. Place remaining icing in small resealable plastic food storage bag. Cut off small corner of bag for piping.

5 Decorate animals and fence sections with icing and assorted candies according to photo. Cover 20-inch piece of cardboard with decorative paper and plastic wrap. Assemble fence by piping icing on bottom and side edges of fence sections. Use smaller sections to make 2 gates. Pipe icing on feet of animals; arrange so animals can be supported by fence or other animals. Sprinkle green-tinted coconut around feet of animals for grass, if desired.

Makes 1 fence and 2 dozen animals

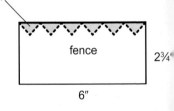

Shapers

What you need:

2 packages (20 ounces each) refrigerated sugar cookie dough
Red, yellow, green and blue paste food colors

DECORATIONS
1 container vanilla frosting

1 Remove dough from wrapper according to package directions. Cut each roll of dough in half.

2 Beat ¼ of dough and red food coloring in medium bowl at medium speed of electric mixer until well blended.

3 Roll red dough on sheet of waxed paper to 5-inch log. Set aside.

4 Repeat with remaining dough and food colors. Cover; refrigerate tinted logs 1 hour or until firm.

5 Working with one log at a time, roll on smooth surface to create circular, triangular, square and oval shaped logs. Use ruler to keep triangle and square sides flat.

6 Cover; refrigerate dough 1 hour or until firm.

7 Preheat oven to 350°F. Cut shaped dough into ¼-inch slices. Place 2 inches apart on ungreased baking sheets.

8 Bake 9 to 12 minutes. Remove to wire racks; cool completely.

9 Spoon frosting into resealable plastic food storage bag; seal. Cut tiny tip from corner of bag.

10 Pipe frosting around each cookie to define shape.
Makes about 6½ dozen cookie

Tip

If you have extra liquid food colors at home, tint the vanilla frosting different colors. Frost cookies using contrasting colored frosting, for example green frosting on a red cookie.

Kaleidoscope Cookies

What you need:

1 package (20 ounces)
   refrigerated sugar
   cookie dough
All-purpose flour
   (optional)
Blue and red liquid
   food colors
2 tablespoons sprinkles,
   multi-colored coarse
   sugar or rock sugar,
   divided

1 Remove dough from wrapper according to package directions. Cut dough into 5 equal sections. Cover and refrigerate 1 section. Sprinkle remaining 4 sections with flour to minimize sticking, if necessary.

2 Add blue food coloring to 1 section in medium bowl; mix using wooden spoon until well blended. Repeat with another section of dough and red food coloring. Roll each section into 7½-inch log. Cover and refrigerate.

3 Add 1 tablespoon sprinkles to third section in medium bowl; mix using wooden spoon until well blended. Repeat with fourth section of dough and remaining 1 tablespoon sprinkles. Roll each section into 7½-inch log. Cover and refrigerate.

4 Roll reserved section of dough on sheet of waxed paper to 7½×8½-inch rectangle. Place logs of dough in middle of rectangle so that matching colors are diagonal from each other.

5 Bring waxed paper and closest edge of dough up and over top of logs. Press gently. Repeat with opposite side, overlapping dough edges. Press gently. Wrap waxed paper around dough and twist ends to secure.

6 Freeze 20 minutes. Preheat oven to 350°F. Grease cookie sheets.

7 Remove waxed paper. Cut log with sharp knife into ½-inch slices. Place 2 inches apart on prepared cookie sheets.

8 Bake 15 to 17 minutes or until edges are lightly browned. Remove to wire racks cool completely.

Makes about 15 cookie

Cookie Bowl and Cookie Fruit

What you need:

1 cup butter or
    margarine, softened
1½ cups sugar
2 whole eggs
2 teaspoons grated
    orange peel
2 teaspoons vanilla
5 cups all-purpose flour
1 teaspoon baking
    powder
½ teaspoon salt
1 cup sour cream

DECORATIONS

4 egg yolks, divided
4 teaspoons water,
    divided
Red, yellow, blue and
    green liquid food
    colors

SUPPLIES

Small craft paint
    brushes

1 Beat butter and sugar in large bowl at high speed of electric mixer until light and fluffy. Add whole eggs, orange peel and vanilla; mix until well blended.

2 Combine flour, baking powder and salt in another large bowl. Add half of flour mixture to butter mixture; mix at low speed until well blended. Add sour cream; mix well. Add remaining flour mixture; mix well.

3 Divide dough into 4 equal sections. Cover; refrigerate several hours or overnight.

4 Place 1 egg yolk in each of 4 separate bowls. Add 1 teaspoon water and food color to each; beat lightly. Set aside.

5 Preheat oven to 375°F. Roll 1 section of dough on well-floured surface to 12-inch circle. Carefully transfer to inverted 1½-quart ovenproof bowl. Press overlapping portions of dough together; trim edges. Paint sides of bowl as desired using small craft paint brushes and egg yolk paint.

6 Place bowl on wire rack and then on cookie sheet. Bake 20 to 25 minutes or until lightly browned. Cool completely on bowl.

7 Roll remaining dough on well-floured surface to ⅛-inch thickness. Cut with fruit shaped cookie cutters. Place 2 inches apart on ungreased cookie sheets. Paint as desired with egg yolk paint.

8 Bake 10 to 12 minutes or until edges are lightly browned. Remove to wire racks; cool completely.

Makes 1 bowl and 4 dozen cookies

Cookie Pops

What you need:

1 package (20 ounces) refrigerated sugar cookie dough
All-purpose flour (optional)

SUPPLIES
20 (4-inch) lollipop sticks

DECORATIONS
Assorted colored sugars, frostings, glazes and gels

1 Preheat oven to 350°F. Grease cookie sheets.

2 Remove dough from wrapper according to package directions.

3 Sprinkle with flour to minimize sticking, if necessary. Cut dough in half.

Reserve 1 half; refrigerate remaining dough.

4 Roll reserved dough to ⅛-inch thickness. Cut out cookies using 3½-inch cookie cutters.

5 Place lollipop sticks on cookies so that tips of sticks are imbedded in cookies. Carefully turn cookies so sticks are in back; place on prepared cookie sheets. Repeat with remaining dough.

6 Bake 7 to 11 minutes or until edges are lightly browned. Cool cookies on cookie sheets 2 minutes. Remove cookies to wire racks; cool completely.

7 Decorate with colored sugars, frostings, glazes and gels as desired.
Makes 20 cookies

Cookie Pops

The Thousand Legged Worm

What you need:

1 package (20 ounces) refrigerated sugar cookie dough
2 containers (16 ounces each) chocolate frosting
Black licorice strings, cut into 3-inch pieces
1 marshmallow and coconut covered chocolate snack cake

DECORATIONS
Miniature round butter cookies and assorted chewy candies

1 Preheat oven to 350°F. Grease cookie sheets.

2 Remove dough from wrapper according to package directions.

3 Cut dough into 30 (½-inch) slices. Place 2 inches apart on prepared cookie sheets.

4 Bake 8 to 10 minutes or until edges are lightly browned. Cool completely on wire racks.

5 Spread underside of 1 cookie with 1 tablespoon frosting. Top with another cookie, pressing gently. Set aside.

6 Spread underside of another cookie with frosting, insert 1 piece of licorice into frosting on each side of cookie and attach to reserved sandwich cookie with frosting.

7 Repeat until 6 cookies are sandwiched together with frosting and licorice.

8 Place cookie stack on its side on serving platter. Repeat with remaining cookies, frosting and licorice.

9 Attach snack cake to 1 end of worm using frosting.

10 Decorate with cookies and assorted candies to resemble face.

Makes 1 worm (3 dozen cookies)

Tip

To make this party worm into a cute birthday worm, insert birthday candles into the frosting used to hold the cookies together. It's sure to be the hit of the party.

Cookie Pizza

What you need:

1 package (20 ounces)
   refrigerated sugar or
   peanut butter cookie
   dough
All-purpose flour
   (optional)
6 ounces (1 cup)
   semisweet chocolate
   chips
1 tablespoon plus
   2 teaspoons
   shortening, divided
¼ cup white chocolate
   chips

TOPPINGS
   Gummy fruit,
   chocolate-covered
   peanuts, assorted
   roasted nuts, raisins,
   jelly beans and other
   assorted candies

1 Preheat oven to 350°F.
Generously grease 12-inch
pizza pan.

2 Remove dough from
wrapper according to
package directions.

3 Sprinkle dough with flour to
minimize sticking, if
necessary. Press dough into
bottom of prepared pan, leaving
about ¾-inch space between
edge of dough and pan.

4 Bake 14 to 23 minutes or
until golden brown and set
in center. Cool completely in pan
on wire rack, running spatula
between cookie crust and pan
after 10 to 15 minutes to loosen.

5 Melt semisweet chocolate
chips and 1 tablespoon
shortening in microwavable
bowl on HIGH (100%) 1 minute;
stir. Repeat process at 10 to
20 second intervals until
smooth.

6 Melt white chocolate chips
and remaining 2 teaspoons
shortening in another
microwavable bowl on
MEDIUM-HIGH (70%) 1 minute;
stir. Repeat process at 10 to
20 second intervals until
smooth.

7 Spread melted semisweet
chocolate mixture over
crust to within 1-inch of edge.
Decorate with desired toppings.

8 Drizzle melted white
chocolate over toppings to
resemble melted mozzarella
cheese. Cut and serve.
   Makes 10 to 12 pizza slices

Name Jewelry

What you need:

1 recipe Christmas Ornament Cookie Dough (page 93)

SUPPLIES
  Plastic drinking straw
  Thin ribbon or yarn

DECORATIONS
  White Icing (recipe follows)
  Colored sugars
  Assorted food colors (optional)
  Small candies (optional)

1 Prepare Christmas Ornament Cookie Dough. Divide dough in half; wrap in plastic wrap. Refrigerate 30 minutes or until firm.

2 Preheat oven to 350°F. Grease cookie sheets.

3 Roll ½ of dough on floured surface to ¼-inch thickness. Cut out cookies using 3¾-inch cookie cutters of various shapes, such as rectangles, circles and hearts.

4 Place cookies on prepared cookie sheets. With plastic straw, make holes in tops of cookies, about ½ inch from top edges.

5 Bake 10 to 12 minutes or until edges begin to brown. Remove cookies to wire racks; cool completely. If necessary, push straw through warm cookies to remake holes.

6 Cut ribbon into 18 (32-inch) pieces. Thread ribbon through holes.

7 Prepare White Icing; spread over cookies. Let stand 40 minutes or until set. Spoon colored or additional icing into small resealable plastic food storage bag. Cut tiny tip from corner of bag. Pipe individual names directly onto cookies as shown in photo. Let stand until set. Decorate with colored sugars and small candies, if desired.

*Makes about 18 cooki
necklace*

White Icing

2 cups powdered sugar
2 tablespoons milk or lemon juice

Combine powdered sugar and milk in small bowl until smooth. (Icing will be very thick. Stir in 1 teaspoon additional milk, if desired.) Icing may be divided into small bowls and tinted with food coloring, if desired.

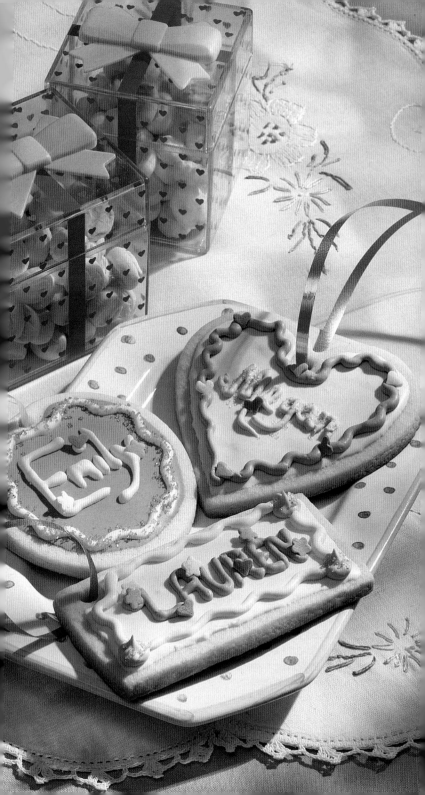

Smushy Cookies

What you need:

1 package (20 ounces) refrigerated cookie dough, any flavor
All-purpose flour (optional)

FILLINGS
Peanut butter, multi-colored miniature marshmallows, assorted colored sprinkles, chocolate-covered raisins and caramel candy squares

1 Preheat oven to 350°F. Grease cookie sheets.

2 Remove dough from wrapper according to package directions.

3 Cut dough into 4 equal sections. Reserve 1 section; refrigerate remaining 3 sections.

4 Roll reserved dough to ¼-inch thickness. Sprinkle with flour to minimize sticking, if necessary.

5 Cut out cookies using 2½-inch round cookie cutter. Transfer to prepared cookie sheets. Repeat with remaining dough.

6 Bake 8 to 11 minutes or until edges are light golden brown. Remove to wire racks; cool completely.

7 To make sandwich, spread about 1½ tablespoons peanut butter on underside of 1 cookie to within ¼ inch of edge. Sprinkle with miniature marshmallows and candy pieces.

8 Top with second cookie, pressing gently. Repeat with remaining cookies and fillings.

9 Just before serving, place sandwiches on paper towels. Microwave on HIGH (100%) 15 to 25 seconds or until fillings become soft.

Makes about 8 to 10 sandwich cookies.

Invite the neighbor kids over on a rainy day to make these fun Smushy Cookies. Be sure to have lots of filling choices avaliable so each child can create their own unique cookies.

Sunshine Butter Cookies

What you need:

¾ cup butter, softened
¾ cup sugar
1 egg
2¼ cups all-purpose flour
¼ teaspoon salt
Grated peel of
    ½ lemon
1 teaspoon frozen
    lemonade
    concentrate, thawed
1 recipe Lemonade
    Royal Icing (page 94)
1 egg, beaten
Thin pretzel sticks
Yellow paste food
    color

DECORATIONS
Gummy fruit and black
    licorice strings

1 Beat butter and sugar in large bowl at high speed of electric mixer until fluffy. Add egg; beat well.

2 Combine flour, salt and lemon peel in medium bowl. Add to butter mixture. Stir in lemonade concentrate. Refrigerate 2 hours.

3 Prepare Lemonade Royal Icing. Cover; let stand at room temperature. Preheat oven to 350°F. Grease cookie sheets.

4 Roll dough on floured surface to ⅛-inch thickness. Cut out cookies usir 3-inch round cookie cutter. Place cookies on prepared cookie sheets. Brush cookies with beaten egg. Arrange pretzel sticks around edge of cookies to resemble sunshine rays; press gently. Bake 10 minutes or until lightly browned. Remove to wire rack: cool completely.

5 Add food color to Lemonade Royal Icing. Spoon about ½ cup icing into resealable plastic food storage bag; seal. Cut tiny tip from corner of bag. Pipe thin circle around underside of each cookie to create outline.

6 Add water, 1 tablespoon a† a time, to remaining icing i bowl, until thick but pourable consistency. Spoon icing in cookie centers staying within outline.

7 Decorate cookies with fruit snacks and licorice as shown in photo. Let stand 1 hour or until dry.
    Makes about 3 dozen cookie

Chocolate Pinwheels

What you need:

1 recipe Chocolate Cookie Dough (page 92)

SUPPLIES
24 wooden popsicle sticks

DECORATIONS
24 (¼-inch) round hard candies or other candies
Assorted colored sugars

1 Prepare Chocolate Cookie Dough. Cover; refrigerate 1 hour or until firm.

2 Preheat oven to 325°F. Grease cookie sheets. Place popsicle sticks 4 inches apart on prepared cookie sheets.

3 Roll dough on floured surface to ¼-inch thickness. Cut out cookies using 3-inch round cookie cutter.

4 Place 1 dough round on end of each wooden stick, pressing down. Cut 4 (1-inch) slits around the edge of each dough round according to diagram.

5 Lift 1 side of each slit, bringing the corner to the center of the cookie and pressing gently. Repeat with remaining dough. Place round candy in center of each pinwheel cookie.

6 Bake 10 minutes or until set. Remove to wire racks; cool completely. Decorate with colored sugars.

Makes 2 dozen cookies

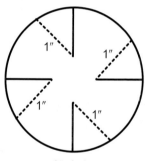

3″ circle

Letters of the Alphabet

What you need:

1 recipe Gingerbread Cookie Dough (page 91)

DECORATIONS
Colored frostings and glazes, colored sugars, sprinkles and assorted small candies

1 Prepare Gingerbread Cookie Dough. Cover; refrigerate about 8 hours or until firm.

2 Preheat oven to 350°F. Grease cookie sheets.

3 Divide dough into 4 equal sections. Reserve 1 section; refrigerate remaining 3 sections.

4 Roll reserved dough on floured surface to ⅛-inch thickness. Sprinkle with flour to minimize sticking, if necessary.

5 Transfer dough to 1 corner of prepared cookie sheet.

6 Cut out alphabet letter shapes using 2½-inch cookie cutters. Repeat steps with remaining dough.

7 Bake 6 to 8 minutes or until edges begin to brown. Remove cookies to wire racks; cool completely.

8 Decorate cookies with frostings, glazes, colored sugars, sprinkles and assorted small candies.
Makes about 5 dozen cookies

Tip

Encourage children to arrange letters to spell names of people they know, their favorite animals or pets, colors or even of places they like to go. A tasty way to learn the ABC's.

YOU'RE INVITED TO A PARTY

Cookie Cups

What you need:

**1 package (20 ounces)
refrigerated sugar
cookie dough
All-purpose flour
(optional)**

FILLINGS
**Prepared pudding,
nondairy whipped
topping, maraschino
cherries, jelly beans,
assorted sprinkles
and small candies**

1 Grease 12 (2¾-inch) muffin cups.

2 Remove dough from wrapper according to package directions. Sprinkle dough with flour to minimize sticking, if necessary.

3 Cut dough into 12 equal pieces; roll into balls. Place 1 ball in bottom of each muffin cup. Press dough halfway up sides of muffin cup, making indentation in center of dough.

4 Freeze muffin cups 15 minutes. Preheat oven to 350°F.

5 Bake 15 to 17 minutes or until golden brown. Cookies will be puffy. Remove from oven; gently press indentation with teaspoon.

6 Return to oven 1 to 2 minutes. Cool cookies in muffin cups 5 minutes. Remove to wire racks; cool completely.

7 Fill each cookie cup with desired fillings. Decorate as desired.

Makes 12 cookie cups

**Giant Cookie Cups
Variation:** Grease 10 (3¾-inch) muffin cups. Cut dough into 10 pieces; roll into balls. Complete recipe according to regular Cookie Cup directions. Makes 10 giant cookie cups.

Tip

Add some pizzazz to your cookie cups by filling with a mixture of prepared fruit-flavored gelatin combined with prepared pudding or nondairy whipped topping. For convenience, snack-size gelatins and puddings can be found at the supermarket, so there is no need to make them from scratch.

JUST
FOR
YOU

Festive Easter Cookies

What you need:

- 1 cup butter or margarine, softened
- 2 cups powdered sugar
- 1 egg
- 2 teaspoons grated lemon peel
- 1 teaspoon vanilla
- 3 cups all-purpose flour
- ½ teaspoon salt
- 1 recipe Royal Icing (page 94)

DECORATIONS

Assorted food colors, icings and candies

1 Beat butter and sugar in large bowl at high speed of electric mixer until fluffy. Add egg, lemon peel and vanilla; mix well. Combine flour and salt in medium bowl. Add to butter mixture; mix well.

2 Divide dough into 2 sections. Cover with plastic wrap. Refrigerate 3 hours or overnight.

3 Preheat oven to 375°F. Roll dough on floured surface to ⅛-inch thickness. Cut out cookies using Easter cookie cutters, such as eggs, bunnies and tulips. Place on ungreased cookie sheets.

4 Bake 8 to 12 minutes or just until edges are very lightly browned. Remove to wire racks; cool completely. Prepare Royal Icing. Decorate as desired. Let stand until icing is set.

Makes 4 dozen cookies

Festive Easter Cookies

Festive Easter Cookies

What you need:

1 cup butter or
    margarine,
    softened
2 cups powdered
    sugar
1 egg
2 teaspoons grated
    lemon peel
1 teaspoon vanilla
3 cups all-purpose
    flour
½ teaspoon salt
1 recipe Royal Icing
    (page 94)

DECORATIONS
    Assorted food
        colors, icings and
        candies

1 Beat butter and sugar in
large bowl at high speed
of electric mixer until fluffy.
Add egg, lemon peel and

vanilla; mix well. Combine
flour and salt in medium
bowl. Add to butter mixture;
mix well.

2 Divide dough into
2 sections. Cover with
plastic wrap. Refrigerate
3 hours or overnight.

3 Preheat oven to 375°F.
Roll dough on floured
surface to ⅛-inch thickness.
Cut out cookies using Easter
cookie cutters, such as eggs,
bunnies and tulips. Place on
ungreased cookie sheets.

4 Bake 8 to 12 minutes or
just until edges are very
lightly browned. Remove to
wire racks; cool completely.
Prepare Royal Icing.
Decorate as desired. Let
stand until icing is set.
        Makes 4 dozen cookies

Festive Easter Cookies

Chocolate and Peanut Butter Hearts

What you need:

1 recipe Chocolate Cookie Dough (page 92)
½ cup creamy peanut butter
½ cup shortening
1 cup sugar
1 egg
1 teaspoon vanilla
3 tablespoons milk
2 cups all-purpose flour
1 teaspoon baking powder
¼ teaspoon salt

1 Prepare Chocolate Cookie Dough. Divide dough in half; wrap in plastic wrap. Refrigerate about 2 hours or until firm.

2 Beat peanut butter, shortening and sugar at medium speed of electric mixer until fluffy. Add egg and vanilla; mix until well blended. Add milk; mix well.

3 Combine flour, baking powder and salt in medium bowl. Add flour mixture to peanut butter mixture; mix at low speed until well blended. Divide dough in half; wrap in plastic wrap. Refrigerate 1 to 2 hours or until firm.

4 Preheat oven to 350°F. Grease cookie sheets. Ro ½ of peanut butter dough on floured waxed paper to ⅛-inch thickness. Cut out cookies usin 3-inch heart-shaped cookie cutter. Place on prepared cooki sheets.

5 Use smaller heart-shaped cookie cutter to remove small section from center of heart; set smaller cutouts aside

6 Repeat with chocolate dough. Place small hearts into opposite dough according to photo; press lightly.

7 Bake 12 to 14 minutes or until edges are lightly browned. Remove to wire racks cool completely.

Makes 4 dozen cookie

Chocolate and Peanut Butter Hearts

Angels

What you need:

1 recipe Butter Cookie Dough (page 92)
1 egg, lightly beaten

DECORATIONS

Small pretzels, white frosting, toasted coconut, glitter dust and assorted small decors

1 Prepare Butter Cookie Dough. Refrigerate about 6 hours or until firm.

2 Preheat oven to 350°F. Grease cookie sheets. Roll dough on floured surface to ¼-inch thickness.

3 Cut out 12 (4-inch) triangles according to diagram. Reroll scraps to ¼-inch thickness. Cut out 12 (1½-inch) circles according to diagram.

4 Place triangles on prepared cookie sheets. Brush tops with beaten egg. Attach circle, pressing gently.

5 Bake 8 to 10 minutes or just until edges begin to brown. Remove to wire racks; cool completely.

6 Attach pretzels to back of each cookie for wings using frosting as "glue". Let dry 30 minutes. Pipe frosting around hairline of each angel; sprinkle with coconut and glitter dust.

7 Pipe frosting on body of cookie to resemble arms and gown. Decorate faces as desired. Let stand 1 hour or until dry.

Makes 1 dozen cookies

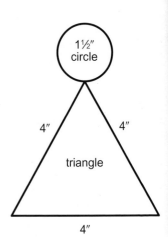

Christmas Tree Platter

What you need:

1 recipe Christmas Ornament Cookie Dough (page 93)
2 cups sifted powdered sugar
2 tablespoons milk or lemon juice

DECORATIONS
Assorted food colors, colored sugars and assorted small decors

1 Preheat oven to 350°F. Prepare Christmas Ornament Cookie Dough. Divide dough in half. Reserve 1 half; refrigerate remaining dough. Roll reserved half of dough to ⅛-inch thickness.

2 Cut out tree shapes with cookie cutters. Place on ungreased cookie sheets.

3 Bake 10 to 12 minutes or until edges are lightly browned. Remove to wire racks; cool completely.

4 Repeat with remaining half of dough. Reroll scraps; cut into small circles for ornaments, squares and rectangles for gift boxes and tree trunks.

5 Bake 8 to 12 minutes, depending on size of cookies.

6 Mix sugar and milk for icing. Tint most of icing green and a smaller amount red or other colors for ornaments and boxes. Spread green icing on trees. Sprinkle ornaments and boxes with colored sugars or decorate as desired.

7 Arrange cookies on flat platter to resemble tree as shown in photo.

Makes about 1 dozen cookie

Tip

Use this beautiful Christmas Tree Platter cookie as your centerpiec for this holiday's family dinner. It' sure to receive lots of "oohs" and "ahs"!

Snowmen

What you need:

**1 package (20 ounces)
refrigerated
chocolate chip
cookie dough
1½ cups sifted powdered
sugar
2 tablespoons milk**

DECORATIONS
**Candy corn, gum
drops, chocolate
chips, licorice and
other assorted small
candies**

1 Preheat oven to 375°F.

2 Cut dough into 12 equal
sections. Divide each
section into 3 balls: large,
medium and small for each
snowman.

3 For each snowman, place
3 balls in a row, ¼ inch
apart, on ungreased cookie
sheet. Repeat with remaining
dough.

4 Bake 10 to 12 minutes or
until edges are very lightly
browned.

5 Cool 4 minutes on cookie
sheets. Remove to wire
racks; cool completely.

6 Mix powdered sugar and
milk in medium bowl until
smooth. Pour over cookies. Let
cookies stand 20 minutes or
until set.

7 Decorate to create faces,
hats and arms with
assorted candies.

Makes 1 dozen cookie

Tip

*Create your own holiday village
by baking several batches of
Snowmen, Angels (page 82)
and Gingerbread Cookie
(page 88).*

Gingerbread Log Cabin

7 cups all-purpose flour
1 tablespoon plus
1½ teaspoons
ground ginger
2 teaspoons baking
soda
¼ teaspoons ground
allspice
1¼ teaspoons salt
2⅔ cups packed brown
sugar
1⅓ cups butter or
margarine, softened
1 cup dark corn syrup
3 eggs

SUPPLIES
Cardboard
Aluminum foil

DECORATIONS
Royal Icing (page 94)
Assorted food colors
Assorted gum drops
and hard candies

1 Draw patterns for house on cardboard, using diagrams on page 90; cut out patterns. Preheat oven to 375°F. Grease and flour large cookie sheet. Combine flour, ginger, baking soda, allspice and salt in medium bowl.

2 Beat brown sugar and butter in large bowl at medium speed of electric mixer until fluffy. Beat in corn syrup and eggs. Gradually add 6 cups of flour mixture to brown sugar mixture. Beat until well blended. Stir in remaining flour mixture with wooden spoon. Divide dough into 4 equal sections. Reserve 1 section; refrigerate remaining 3 sections.

3 To make sides of cabin, roll reserved dough directly onto prepared cookie sheet to ¼-inch thickness. Lay sheet of waxed paper over dough. Place patterns over waxed paper 2 inches apart. Cut dough around pattern with sharp knife; remove patterns and waxed paper. Reserve scraps to reroll with next section of dough.

4 To make logs, roll dough into 12 (1-inch) balls. Roll each ball into 6-inch rope. Lay 6 logs parallel to one another on 1 prepared house side, leaving ¼-inch border at top and bottom of house side. Repeat steps with remaining 6 balls and second side. Freeze 15 minutes.

5 Bake 15 to 18 minutes or until no indentation remains when cookies are touched in center. While cookies are still hot, place cardboard pattern lightly over cookies; trim edges with sharp knife to straighten. Return to oven 2 minutes. Let stand on cookie sheets 5 *continued*

Gingerbread Log Cabin, continued

minutes. Remove using spatula to wire racks; cool completely. Leave cookie pieces out uncovered overnight.

6 To make front and back walls, repeat step 3. To make logs for front and back, roll dough into 18 (1¼-inch) balls. Roll each ball into 7-inch log. Place 9 logs for front wall over cardboard pattern as a guide; cut out openings for windows. Lay logs parallel on front wall, leaving ¼-inch border at top and bottom of wall. Repeat steps with remaining 9 balls and back wall. Freeze 15 minutes. Bake and reserve as directed in step 5.

7 To make roof, repeat step 3. To make logs for roof, roll dough into 16 (1¼-inch) balls. Roll each ball into 7½-inch log. Lay logs parallel to one another on roof, leaving ¼-inch border at top and bottom of roof. Freeze 15 minutes. Bake and reserve as directed in step 5.

8 To make chimney, roll cookie scraps into ball. Roll

and cut out rectangle about 3×1¾-inches. Bake 10 to 12 minutes.

9 Cover 15-inch square piece of heavy cardboard with foil to use as base for cabin. Prepare Royal Icing. Place icing in small resealable plastic food storage bag. Cut off small corner of bag. Pipe icing on edges of all pieces including bottom; "glue" house together a seams and on base.

10 Position mug against outside of each wall and another at inside corner where 2 walls meet. Let dry at least 6 hours. When icing is set, remove mugs from inside walls. Pipe icing onto roof edges and attach to house. Place mug under each side of roof. Let dry at least 6 hours. Decorate with additional icing and candies as desired. Place chimney near to of one side of roof; attach with icing.

11 Pipe icing on cabin to resemble snow. Decorate as desired.
Makes 1 gingerbread log cabin

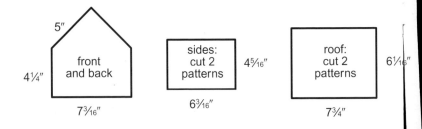

*Yield and baking times have not been included
for these cookies. For best results, prepare and bake as
directed in individual recipes.*

Gingerbread Cookie Dough

What you need:

½ **cup shortening**
⅓ **cup packed light brown sugar**
¼ **cup dark molasses**
1 **egg white**
½ **teaspoon vanilla**
1½ **cups all-purpose flour**
1 **teaspoon ground cinnamon**
½ **teaspoon baking soda**
½ **teaspoon salt**
½ **teaspoon ground ginger**
¼ **teaspoon baking powder**

1 Beat shortening, brown sugar, molasses, egg white and vanilla in large bowl at high speed of electric mixer until smooth.

2 Combine flour, cinnamon, baking soda, salt, ginger and baking powder in small bowl. Add to shortening mixture; mix well. Cover; refrigerate about 8 hours or until firm.

Butter Cookie Dough

What you need:

¾ cup butter or
   margarine, softened
¼ cup granulated sugar
¼ cup packed light
   brown sugar
1 egg yolk
1¾ cups all-purpose flour
¾ teaspoon baking
   powder
⅛ teaspoon salt

1 Combine butter, granulated sugar, brown sugar and egg yolk in medium bowl. Add flour, baking powder and salt; mix well.

2 Cover; refrigerate about 4 hours or until firm.

Chocolate Cookie Dough

What you need:

1 cup butter or
   margarine, softened
1 cup sugar
1 egg
1 teaspoon vanilla
2 ounces semisweet
   chocolate, melted
2¼ cups all-purpose flour
1 teaspoon baking
   powder
¼ teaspoon salt

1 Beat butter and sugar in large bowl at high speed of electric mixer until fluffy. Beat in egg and vanilla. Add melted chocolate; mix well.

2 Add flour, baking powder and salt; mix well. Cover; refrigerate about 2 hours or until firm.

Christmas Ornament Cookie Dough

What you need:

2¼ cups all-purpose flour
¼ teaspoon salt
1 cup sugar
¾ cup butter or
    margarine, softened
1 egg
1 teaspoon vanilla
1 teaspoon almond
    extract

1 Combine flour and salt in medium bowl.

2 Beat sugar and butter in large bowl at medium speed of electric mixer until fluffy. Beat in egg, vanilla and almond extract. Gradually add flour mixture. Beat at low speed until well blended.

3 Form dough into 2 discs; wrap in plastic wrap and refrigerate 30 minutes or until firm.

Gingerbread House Dough

What you need:

5¼ cups all-purpose flour
1 tablespoon ground
    ginger
2 teaspoons baking
    soda
1½ teaspoons ground
    allspice
1 teaspoon salt
2 cups packed dark
    brown sugar
1 cup butter or
    margarine, softened
¾ cup dark corn syrup
2 eggs

1 Combine flour, ginger, baking soda, allspice and salt in medium bowl.

2 Beat brown sugar and butter in large bowl at medium speed of electric mixer until fluffy. Beat in corn syrup and eggs. Gradually add flour mixture. Beat at low speed until well blended. Cover; refrigerate about 2 hours or until firm.

Royal Icing

What you need:

1 egg white, at room
     temperature
2 to 2½ cups sifted
     powdered sugar
½ teaspoon almond
     extract

1 Beat egg white in small bowl
at high speed of electric
mixer until foamy.

2 Gradually add 2 cups
powdered sugar and
almond extract. Beat at low
speed until moistened. Increase
mixer speed to high and beat
until icing is stiff.

Lemonade Royal Icing

What you need:

3¾ cups sifted powdered
     sugar
3 tablespoons meringue
     powder
6 tablespoons frozen
     lemonade
     concentrate, thawed

Beat all ingredients in large bowl
at high speed of electric mixer
until smooth.

Cookie Glaze

What you need:

4 cups powdered sugar
4 to 6 tablespoons milk

Combine powdered sugar and
enough milk, one tablespoon a
a time, to make a medium-thick
pourable glaze.

METRIC CONVERSION CHART

VOLUME MEASUREMENTS (dry)

1/8 teaspoon = 0.5 mL
1/4 teaspoon = 1 mL
1/2 teaspoon = 2 mL
3/4 teaspoon = 4 mL
1 teaspoon = 5 mL
1 tablespoon = 15 mL
2 tablespoons = 30 mL
1/4 cup = 60 mL
1/3 cup = 75 mL
1/2 cup = 125 mL
2/3 cup = 150 mL
3/4 cup = 175 mL
1 cup = 250 mL
2 cups = 1 pint = 500 mL
3 cups = 750 mL
4 cups = 1 quart = 1 L

VOLUME MEASUREMENTS (fluid)

1 fluid ounce (2 tablespoons) = 30 mL
4 fluid ounces (1/2 cup) = 125 mL
8 fluid ounces (1 cup) = 250 mL
12 fluid ounces (1 1/2 cups) = 375 mL
16 fluid ounces (2 cups) = 500 mL

WEIGHTS (mass)

1/2 ounce = 15 g
1 ounce = 30 g
3 ounces = 90 g
4 ounces = 120 g
8 ounces = 225 g
10 ounces = 285 g
12 ounces = 360 g
16 ounces = 1 pound = 450 g

DIMENSIONS

1/16 inch = 2 mm
1/8 inch = 3 mm
1/4 inch = 6 mm
1/2 inch = 1.5 cm
3/4 inch = 2 cm
1 inch = 2.5 cm

OVEN TEMPERATURES

250°F = 120°C
275°F = 140°C
300°F = 150°C
325°F = 160°C
350°F = 180°C
375°F = 190°C
400°F = 200°C
425°F = 220°C
450°F = 230°C

BAKING PAN SIZES

Utensil	Size in Inches/Quarts	Metric Volume	Size in Centimeters
Baking or Cake Pan (square or rectangular)	8×8×2	2 L	20×20×5
	9×9×2	2.5 L	23×23×5
	12×8×2	3 L	30×20×5
	13×9×2	3.5 L	33×23×5
Loaf Pan	8×4×3	1.5 L	20×10×7
	9×5×3	2 L	23×13×7
Round Layer Cake Pan	8×1½	1.2 L	20×4
	9×1½	1.5 L	23×4
Pie Plate	8×1¼	750 mL	20×3
	9×1¼	1 L	23×3
Baking Dish or Casserole	1 quart	1 L	—
	1½ quart	1.5 L	—
	2 quart	2 L	—